SAMMY PLEASE

WASH YOUR

HANDS

SAMMY PLEASE WASH YOUR HANDS

By Samuel Browne

Published by NGOWE

www.ngowe.com

Tampa, Florida, 33611

1st Edition: 2016

ISBN: 978-0-9983204-1-0

Illustrated by
Bassey B. Inyang

Charles. E. Chukukere

DEDICATED TO

All the Ebola Virus Victims, the poor, and the sick and suffering.

ACKNOWLEDGEMENTS

The author wishes to thank God for blessing him with wonderful encouraging parents because they inspire him to aim high, achieve beyond all expectations, think outside the box, and aim to the sky because of its endless possibilities. He also thanks them for exposing him to so many wonderful experiences living in America, the U.S. Virgin Islands, West Africa, and Israel. He also wants to thank all of his teachers during his journey thus far because they helped to shape him into the young man he is today.

INTRODUCTION

"Sammy Please Wash Your Hands" by Yasad Samuel Browne is a part of the Sammy Series. In this book, Sammy learns the importance of washing his to prevent the spread of disease. The author decided to write this book when he was in Nigeria West Africa during the Ebola Virus crisis. He remembers the scare, precaution, and anxiety everyone felt as Africa went on high alert to stop the spread of Ebola.

Handwashing with soap and water was an important tool used to prevent the spread of the Ebola Virus and it is critical for protecting against things like the cold, flu, germs, diseases, viruses, and food-borne illnesses. Today he reflects on the comforts we take for granted in America and reflects on the poverty and struggles seen in the poor communities in Africa. So young to see so much and know that he has to be an agent of change with the purpose in life to make a difference.

Sammy ran outside to play

He played and played and played.
He played in the dirt

He played in the drain

He played with the cow, and

rode the horse to the pen,

chased the roach out the den,

and got chased by a goat
round the bend.

That silly Sammy!

YEP!!!

You got it,

Sammy loves to

play,

and play,

and play.

Sammy never wants to stop playing, he even tries to play in the rain.

Sammy it's raining, get inside right now, you can get hurt. Sammy look at the lighting.

GET

INSIDE

RIGHT

NOW!!!"

Mommy yelled with fear.

When it was time to do his chores he helps feed the cow and the goat

And helps his Dad with the chickens and the hens

Its lunchtime now and Mamma called

"SAMMY!!!

SAMMY!!!

SAMMY!!!"

SAMMY!!!"

Sammy came running like he was being chased by the mule in the pen!

He went to the table, wipes his hands on his napkin and began to pray.

"Thank you for the food we eat
Thank you for the goat and sheep

Thank you for grandpa in heaven

Thank you for making me seven

Thank you for the God above

Thank you for looking at us with love.

AMEN."

Right then Sammy began to eat.

"Sammy, did you wash your hands???" Mama asked

"Yes Mama I cleaned them"

"You cleaned them, but did you use soap to wash them properly?"

Sammy looked down at his hand, saw the dirt and replied

"No Mama."

Time passed by and he got sick

So in the hospital he was, taking time to think.

It was not
worth to hide
the dirt,
now his
body hurt
and
hurt

Doctor Bob told him
"Washing your hands
will help to keep you well;
it will protect you from germs,
and stop
diseases,
viruses, and
food-borne illnesses
from
spreading"

Mom said in a frightened voice "Sammy I love you so much my dear, I clean the house to keep you safe. However, poor hand washing can expose you to things like the cold, flue, and some illnesses you can even die from, the Ebola virus, swine flu from chickens and mad cow disease from the cows to name a few; that's why you need to wash your hands all the time to protect yourself."

Oh God save us I pray!"

Sammy got well and he went home and back to playing in the dirt.

It was time to eat and Mama reminded Sammy "Wash your hands before eating, after using the bathroom, touching money and uncooked meat, taking care of the animals, playing with your pets, blowing your nose, sneezing, coughing, taking out the trash, and playing in the dirt."

"Come right now to the sink,
I'll teach
you to wash your hands
properly

First wet
your hands to loosen the dirt
and germs

Then add some soap to kill
the germs that cause those
things that can make you
sick.

Rub your hands together and make a lather, then scrub under your nails and between your fingers for 20 seconds or while singing the Happy Birthday song.

Then rinse very well. Sammy yelled "EEKKK, AW, YUCK, EWW!!! As he looks at the dirt washing away from his hands. "Do you see the dirt?" Mama asked. "Wow that is yucky" he replied scornfully

Next you dry your hands with paper towel, a clean towel, or cloth.

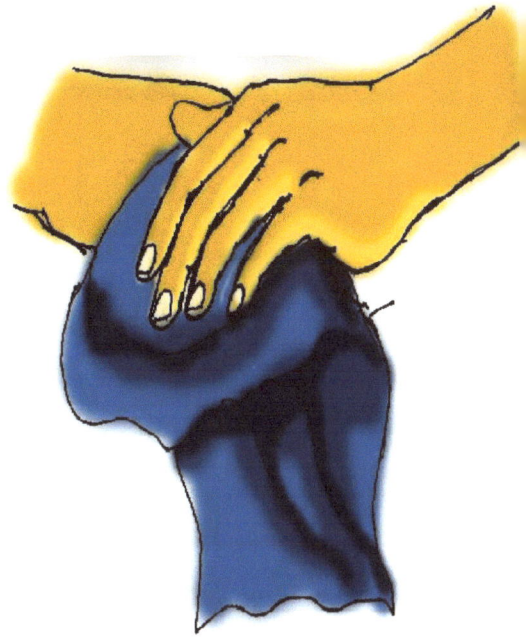

The last thing you do is to turn off the tap. It is better to use a paper towel to turn off the tap to prevent the germs on the tap from getting on your hands.

Sammy is all better now.
He is much wiser and
stronger than before because
he practices good hygiene every
day.
Sammy ran back outside
and did one of his favorite
things, he played,
and played,
and played.

The End

AUTHOR'S BIOGAPHY

Samuel Browne was born in 1999 in Atlanta Georgia but grew up on the beautiful island of St. Croix United States Virgin Island. He grew up an active child involved in soccer, basketball, baseball, tennis, and track and field. However, soccer was his main passion. He is an amazing soccer player and hopes that one day he is discovered by the national soccer team. He currently attends Florida Golf Coast University and plays for the Tampa Bay United U18 Soccer team. At present, his primary interests are education, writing poetry and songs, playing his piano, developing video games, and of course playing soccer. His creativity and passion for life allow him to look deep within himself to write. His ambition in life is to be the best he could be and become an inspiration to others.

www.YasadBrowne.com

MORE BOOKS AND NOVELS AVAILABLE FROM NGOWE

Life To Me
Sammy Learns His A B C
Sammy Learns to Read at 3
Sammy Please Wash Your Hands
Melissa Against the World
The Sketcher

www.ingramcontent.com/pod-product-compliance
Lightning Source LLC
Chambersburg PA
CBHW041553040426
42447CB00002B/165